Walks

Text: *Chiz Dakin*

Series editor: *Tony Bowerman*

Photographs: *Chiz Dakin, Carl Rogers, Alamy, ,Adobe Stock, Dreamstime, Shutterstock*

Design: *Carl Rogers and Laura Hodgkinson*

© *Northern Eye Books Limited 2021*

Chiz Dakin has asserted her rights under the Copyright, Designs and Patents Act, 1988 to be identified as the author of this work. All rights reserved.

This book contains mapping data licensed from the Ordnance Survey with the permission of the Controller of Her Majesty's Stationery Office. © Crown copyright 2021. All rights reserved. License number 100047867

Northern Eye Books

ISBN 978-1-908632-79-1

A CIP catalogue record for this book is available from the British Library.

Printed in the UK

www.northerneyebooks.co.uk

Cover: *Three Roofs Cafe, Castleton (Walk 10)*

First published in 2019. This edition published in 2021 by:

Northern Eye Books Limited
Northern Eye Books, Tattenhall, Cheshire CH3 9PX

tony@northerneyebooks.com

www.northerneyebooks.co.uk

 @northerneyebooks

@northerneyeboo

For sales enquiries, please call: 01928 723744

MIX
Paper from responsible sources
FSC® C016379

Contents

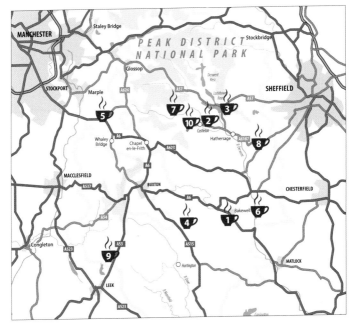

England's First National Park

CREATED IN 1951, THE PEAK DISTRICT NATIONAL PARK extends over six counties and is the second most visited of Britain's National Parks. Its highest point lies upon the seemingly remote Kinder Plateau, where a mass trespass in 1932 marked the turning point in a long and sometimes bitter campaign that led to the creation of Britain's National Parks and the open access we enjoy today.

The high, peaty moorlands of the northern Dark Peak are founded on gritstone, their stark grandeur accentuated by impressive weatherworn tors and edges. The moors extend out of the Pennines in two horns that enclose the limestone plateau of the White Peak, an upland pasture cleft by narrow gorges and dales. The transition between the two is startlingly abrupt and each has a distinctive character and beauty all its own; the wild openness of the north contrasting with the south's intimate landscape dotted with small villages and criss-crossed by old lanes.

Sunrise and mist at Winnats Pass, near Castleton

Cafés, Tea Shops and Tea Rooms

For many of us, the feeling that we've earned a treat is one of the reasons for walking in the first place. Home-made cakes (with many cafés now offering fabulous gluten-free options too) usually hit the mark whatever the season, but in winter nothing beats the hand-and-body-warming effect of a good mug of freshly brewed coffee or tea, or a bowl of hearty soup. Come summer, it may be a glass of the local ale or a frosty tub of local ice-cream that hits the mark for cooling down after enjoying the fresh air. And sometimes nothing else will do but a light snack or even a full meal.

"Yes, that's it," said the Hatter with a sigh,
"It's always tea time..."

Lewis Carroll

TOP 10 **Walks:** Cafés, Tea Shops and Bistros

THE PEAK DISTRICT ABOUNDS WITH CAFÉS AND TEA SHOPS offering fabulous, freshly brewed coffee and a mouthwatering variety of speciality teas. This pocket-size guide picks carefully selected cafés across the Peak District — in locations ranging from former stations to community cafés, National Trust properties to hillside farms, and cafés on town streets to tearooms tucked down alleyways. All of them offer a great choice of often home-baked or locally sourced produce, and a pleasant place to relax after a refreshing walk.

Hassop Station, Bakewell

page 8

Café Adventure, Hope

page 12

Anglers' Rest Café, Bamford

page 18

The Old Smithy, Monyash

page 24

Hassop Station is now a popular café on the Monsal Trail near Bakewell

BAKEWELL

Hassop Station Café

An easy-going walk over rolling hillside paths and tracks following an old turnpike and former railway line

What to expect:
Grassy riverside path and meadow, gentle rolling hills, Monsal Trail, busy road crossing in Bakewell

Distance/Time: 5 kilometres/ 3 miles. Allow 2 hours

Start: Bakewell Station, Bakewell DE45 1NW

Grid Ref: SK 222 689

Ordnance Survey Map: Explorer OL24 Peak District: White Peak area: *Buxton, Bakewell, Matlock & Dovedale*

After the Walk: Hassop Station Bookshop Café and Cycle Hire, Hassop Station, DE45 1NW | 01629 815 668 | www.hassopstation.co.uk

Walk outline: From Bakewell's former railway station, a short stroll leads down to the riverbank, then along this to the old Newcastle Under Lyme to Hassop Hall Turnpike route. Rise out of Bakewell on this over a couple of gentle hills to the Monsal Trail — a former rail line now converted to a multi-use easy going track. The café is just along the track, which then leads easily back to the parking at the top of Bakewell.

This former station turned café-bookshop and cycle hire centre offers an excellent cup of coffee, hot meals with local wine or beer and a range of soft drinks. At the counter is a delicious display of cakes, but the sausage cobs are among the best in the Peak District.

Friendly staff

▶ Hassop Station Café at a glance

Open: 09.00-17.00, 7 days a week, 362 days a year (Additional late opening in summer)

Food and Specialities: Homemade cakes, toasties, soup to full meals. Breakfast baps, fresh local beef burgers and station platters. Gluten free and vegan options for cakes. Food is locally sourced where possible

Beverages: Fresh Barista-style coffee, range of teas and speciality teas, bottled soft drinks, bottled ale from Peak Ales and Thornbridge, wine

Outside: Picnic tables and sun terrace above the Monsal Trail. Large outdoor covered area. Wood-fired pizza oven for summer evenings

The Walk

1. From the **car park**, head down **Station Road** to a T-junction by the **Derwent River bridge**, on the edge of Bakewell. Cross the **A619** and take a lovely, easy-going cinder trail through a metal gate to **Scot's Garden**. This meanders next to the riverbank then cuts across a corner of meadow. Go through two gates as the river bends back to the path, then follow red-lined waymarkers across a small field to a residential lane.

2. Turn left onto this and follow it to the end of the public road (by **Riverside Business Park**). Turn right onto a gravel track, passing a blue plaqued house where Richard Arkwright Jnr once lived. The surface briefly roughens and steepens through **woodland**, then enters a grassy field. Rise up on the continuation vehicle track until it branches left, then maintain your direction to the top of the field.

3. A **green lane** now undulates over two low hills to **Hassop Station**. It seems to become greener as you top the first rise and begin a gentle descent between pasture fields. The second rise is barely perceptible; passage through three gates fairly close together is about as much indication as you get. The path narrows somewhat after the third gate, with summer undergrowth often encroaching.

This green lane was once the main turnpike, or toll road, between Newcastle-under-Lyme and Hassop Hall. Look out for an old cottage across the fields as it ends at the Monsal

An undulating green lane winds between Bakewell and Hassop

Trail — this was a Toll House during its turnpike days.

4. Exit rightwards onto the **Monsal Trail** and follow this for about 400 metres along the former railway line to an **overbridge**.

5. Just beyond the bridge, turn left for the **café** at **Hassop Station**.

Once refreshed, it's now about 1.6 kilometres/1 mile along the **Monsal Trail** back to the start, passing under a road-bridge on the way. Go past a few industrial buildings on the right, and then turn right immediately before the **former station buildings** on a narrow cut-through to the car park to complete the walk. ♦

Stately stations?
The two stations of Bakewell and Hassop are a curious anomaly illustrating power and privilege. Although neither are central to the town, both could equally serve as its main station. Curiously, Bakewell station was built for the benefit of the Duke of Rutland and his Haddon Hall Estate (and bears his coat of arms in the walls); while Hassop station was built for the convenience of the Duke of Devonshire and his Chatsworth Estate.

Cafe ADVENTURE

Freshly cooked
Homemade Food
Breakfast
Lunch
Coffee
Cakes
Bistro Nights

Enjoy superb coffee and cake at the Adventure Café, Hope

Café Adventure

A strenuous walk with views over the Derwent Reservoirs from the grassy ridgeline and rocky summit knoll

What to expect:
Steep ascent/descent, bracken-covered hillside, rocky summit, grassy ridgeline

Distance/Time: 8 kilometres/ 5 miles. Allow 3½ hours

Start: Hope village car park. Pay and Display

Grid Ref: SK 171 835

Ordnance Survey Map: Explorer OL1 The Peak District: Dark Peak area, *Kinder Scout, Bleaklow, Black Hill and Ladybower Reservoir*

After the Walk: Café Adventure, Hope, S33 6ZF | 01433 623313 | www.caféadventure.co.uk

Walk outline: A gentle start to the walk leads to a sustained ascent diagonally up the hillside. This is the easiest way up Win Hill and offers a lovely 2 kilometre, easy stroll along a fantastic ridgeline. The summit is well guarded by outcrops of rock, but a way sneaks through the side of the summit mound. Enjoy the 360 degree panorama from the top, retrace your steps a short distance, then enjoy a fast descent back to Hope.

An outdoors-friendly café, popular with walkers and cyclists alike. Weekend mornings can be very busy before folks set out for a day's walk/ride, likewise afternoons. Fab breakfast burgers and paninis, excellent coffee and tea, plus home-made cakes baked on site.

Cyclists and walkers welcome

▶ Café Adventure at a glance

Open: Daily, 09.00–17.00, closed Tuesdays

Food and specialities: Homemade cakes, breakfast baps, paninis, and salads, with locally sourced ingredients where possible. Wide choice for vegetarians, gluten- and dairy-free diets catered for. Fresh ice cream. Take-away available

Beverages: Fresh barista coffee, English Breakfast and range of speciality teas, luxury hot chocolate; apple and orange juice; specialist soft drinks (Belvoir Presse), milkshakes and smoothies

Outside: Outside tables (café only). Popular with cyclists and walkers

The Walk

1. Opposite the **car park**, take a footpath just right of the **Grasshopper café**.
This leads up steps, past a meadow and through a snicket to a residential road. Follow this to a T-junction, cross the road and enter a small field.

Hope is a rarity in Derbyshire for having not changed its name in over 1000 years. It was mentioned in the Domesday book as having a church and a priest, suggesting it was a place of high importance at the time. This perhaps is down to its location within a large Royal Forest (a medieval Royal hunting reserve) and also at the crossing of two ancient trade routes.

2. At the end of this field, take a footpath right and down to the road.

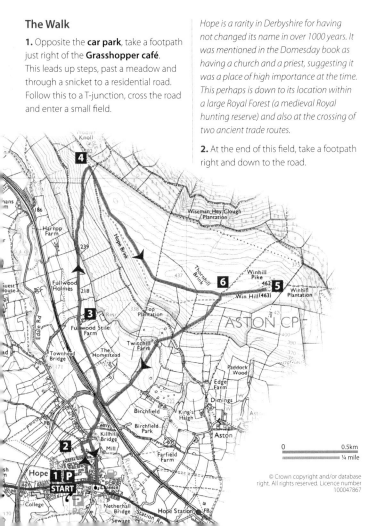

Looking back to the summit from the descent below Thornhill Brink

Cross over onto **Bowden Lane** and follow tarmac to **The Homestead**, bearing left just after the **railway bridge**. A vehicle track leads to **Hope Cottage**, along the top edge of grassy fields, then across a wall by a barn at **Fullwood Stile Farm**, where you follow signs out to **Brinks Road**.

This lane is on the line of the prehistoric Portway, later adopted as a Roman road. It later became a medieval packhorse route used by packhorse drivers called 'jaggers', ferrying salt and other goods between Derbyshire and the salt pans of Cheshire.

When the Romans were using it, it would have formed an important route northwards from their fortress at Navio, whose remains are just south of Hope village in the modern day village of Brough.

3. Rise gently along this lane to access land at a metal gate, then fork right and diagonally uphill through bracken. Pass a former gatepost then, staying on the main grassy track, bend right to a ridge top junction.

4. Follow the ridgeline track rightwards; it's about 2 kilometres of easy walking, bending in a gentle arc up to the summit.

The rocky summit of Win Hill overlooks Ladybower Reservoir

Approaching the summit mound, fork left onto the partly pitched ridgeline track, rising up to the far end of the summit ridge. Turn back along the ridge-top to gain the true trig point summit.

From the summit of Win Hill there's a fabulous panoramic view stretching northwards over Ladybower Reservoir, west and south across the Edale and Hope valleys and eastwards to Lose Hill.

As you look north over Ladybower reservoir, try to imagine it's a dark night in 1943. The roar of approaching aeroplane engines fills the valley as an RAF squadron of Lancaster bombers flies low level over the water towards the massive dam wall at the far

end. Hard to imagine in the warmth of a summer's day, but the Upper Derwent Valley was the prime practice location for 617 squadron ahead of the famous Second World War 'Dambusters' raid.

5. Now retrace your steps back down to a green sign above a gate.

6. Head gently downhill to a **cairn** on a ruined **drystone wall**. Bend left, now descending much more steeply, and leave access land at a stile. There are a few confusing paths in the next field, but you are heading directly downhill towards **wooden railings**, crossing a farm track on the way.

7. Go through a gate below the railings

and drop steeply to houses and through the gate into the old **farmyard**. A long tarmac driveway leads leftwards and down to a road junction by a **railway bridge**. Turn left under the bridge and over the **river** to a T-junction.

8. Turn left and follow this road into **Hope**. The **Adventure Café** is on your left, shortly before you reach the main road. Turn right at the main road to return to the start and complete the walk ♦

Win or lose?

Win Hill is said to have been the winners' chosen high ground in a battle fought sometime in the 7th Century between the King of Northumbria and the allied Kings of Wessex and Mercia. Legend says the army on Win Hill was hopelessly outnumbered yet still won a famous victory by rolling rocks down on the opposition. The losers' base, just across the Noe Valley, was on ... yes, you've guessed it, Lose Hill.

Relaxing with beer and sandwiches at the Anglers' Rest Café

BAMFORD

Anglers' Rest Café

*Longer, strenuous walk with fabulous views over
Ladybower Reservoir and the Kinder Plateau*

What to expect:
*Steep ascent, boggy
moorland, some faint
paths, stepping stones*

Distance/Time: 10 kilometres/ 6 miles. Allow 4 hours

Start: Bamford

Grid Ref: SK 202 860

Ordnance Survey Map: Explorer OL1 The Peak District: Dark Peak
area, *Kinder Scout, Bleaklow, Black Hill and Ladybower Reservoir*

After the Walk: Anglers Rest café, Main Road, Bamford,
Derbyshire, S33 0DY | 01433 659 317 | www.anglers.rest/cafe/

Walk outline: A longer, lesser known edge walk that's well
worth the fairly strenuous ascent to the ridgeline through
a lovely oak woodland holloway. There are great views over
the Bamford Valley and Ladybower Reservoir, with a series of
long zigzags over moorland and fields that ease the descent
to the village and café. Entertaining stepping stones cross
the river by the mill, before a mostly easy-going return.

*This community-owned café is popular with Bamford residents
and visitors alike. There's a pub at the bottom, a café at the top,
and a post office in between. Be sure to try their quirky sweet and
savoury snack — bacon in a toasted tea cake.*

Lovely coffee

▶ Anglers' Rest Café at a glance

Open: Daily, 09.00-late (Sun from 09.30); café food 09.00-16.00 weekends
— plus pub food in the evening
Food and specialities: Homemade and seasonal food. Hearty breakfasts,
breakfast baps (morning only), lighter bites (jacket potatoes, sandwiches,
soup and paninis) and main meals. Home-made cakes
Beverages: Barista-style freshly ground coffee, range of teas and
speciality teas, hot chocolate, soft drinks (alcoholic drinks from 11.00)
Outside: Picnic tables outside, large car park, cycle friendly area

The Walk

1. Start on the **Derwent Valley Heritage Way** footpath which runs above the road from the **car park** towards **Ladybower**

dam wall. Fork leftwards (red trail) at a path junction opposite the dam wall, and then follow concessionary 'white arrow on black background' waymarkers through the **woodland**, forking right under a **double set of power lines**, left at the edge of woodland then right over a stile into **access land**.

2. Follow the concession path leftwards beside the woodland, then at a slight high point in the wall slant diagonally towards higher ground through an **avenue of trees** (ancient holloway) in lovely oak woodland. *There's a great view as you emerge from the woodland over Ladybower Reservoir towards Win Hill, the Kinder plateau and Derwent Edge — the first of many fine viewpoints on the walk.* Head right at a split in the path on a narrow boggy line, cross a broken drystone wall, then take a steepening loop uphill, remaining within 50 metres of the wall. Turn right just below the **edge** and head back across the wall.

Rainbow and clouds rolling in over Ladybower Reservoir

3. Now follow the edge, which gradually gains a rougher steeper craggy side, for about 1.5 kilometres, with a **lone slabby rock** early on and the **crags at Great Tor** being particularly good viewpoints over Ladybower. As the path begins to descend, the edge begins to fade to gentler slopes before reappearing as a new harder edge some distance to the left.

Stay close to the **original edge-line** with a slightly hard to find kink right then left at an area of **old stoneworkings**, which leads down past a couple of abandoned **millstones** to a broad grassy track through bracken. This descends gently then roughly contours across the hillside towards the high end of the **country lane** below. Shortly before joining the lane, merge right with a path heading steeply down from the upper edge, and over furrowed ground to a stile onto the lane.

4. Turn right and descend to a righthand bend at **Bamford Clough**; continue for another kilometre to the next footpath on the left — at the driveway of "**Thie Veg**". (Bamford Clough has been closed for a few years due to 'an exposed live electrical cable', but should it reopen to

Ladybower Reservoir seen from Bamford Edge at sunset

walkers, this may become a preferable if steep descent).

Cross the driveway end and go over a stile into pasture to continue through several fields to **Bamford**. It's mostly a diagonal path across the hillside, with one field of more direct descent. Veer gently right above housing to a metal gate onto the main road. Turn left along the pavement and into the **village**, with the **café** on the first bend to the right.

5. Continue down to the triangular 'Fidlers Well' junction and look for a pair of **tall stone gateposts** on the right, next to a road sign for 'Old Post Office Row'. Go through these onto 'The

Hollow', which descends to **Bamford Mill**. Follow signs for the 'Touchstone Trail' above the mill buildings; then go left between buildings on a wide gravel path to **stepping stones** and a **wooden footbridge** across the **River Derwent**. Note: This can flood in winter. *The sculpture on the bridge is part of the Touchstone Trail which was designed by residents to commemorate the millennium.*

6. Take a footpath diagonally across fields, which soon merges with a **farm track**. Turn left off the track at a waymarker and walk steeply uphill to the **Thornhill Trail**. *This path was once a private railway line ferrying stone from*

quarries at Grindleford to the construction site when Howden and Derwent Dams were built in the 1900s. The dams were needed to provide water to the ever-increasing populations of Sheffield, Derby, Nottingham and northern Leicestershire.

Turn right onto the trail and walk uphill to the **Ladybower Dam Wall**, crossing a lane by a car park to merge left onto a tarmac track. Cross the dam wall and turn left along the pavement to return to **Heatherdene** to complete the walk. ♦

Bamford Mills

The Bamford Mills were one of the earliest of the Derwent Cotton mills, being originally constructed in 1780 on the site of a former corn mill, then rebuilt after a fire in 1791. The weir was constructed from local stone from Bamford Edge. In 1965, mill use ceased and they were converted for manufacturing electric furnaces. Like many former mills, they have now become residential apartments.

CREAM | CAFE ↘

DAVID PATRICK DRISCOLL
. LICENSED TO SELL ALL INTOXICATING LIQUORS .
FOR CONSUMPTION ON OR OFF THE PREMISES

ICE CREAM

Vanilla	Small £1.70
Toffee Ripple	Large £2.20
Strawberry Ripple	Flake 30p
Chocolate Ripple	Lollies £1.50
Mint Choc Chip	
Rum n' Raisin	

DOGS
AND
MUDDY BOOTS
WELCOME

Tempting chalkboards announce daily choices at The Old Smithy

MONYASH

The Old Smithy

One of the Peak's loveliest limestone dales — featuring the source of the River Lathkill and unusual wildflowers

What to expect:
Steep slopes, country lanes, ridgeline path, short but steep rocky holloway.

Distance/Time: 6.5 kilometres/ 4 miles. Allow 2½ hours

Start: Jack Mere car park on Chapel Street, Monyash. Free (but a donation is appreciated)

Grid ref: SK 148 665

Ordnance Survey Map: Explorer OL24 The Peak District, White Peak area, *Buxton, Bakewell, Matlock and Dovedale*

Café: The Old Smithy, Monyash, DE45 1JH | 01629 810190 | www. oldsmithymonyash.co.uk

Walk outline: Little known Bagshaw Dale leads into the far more famous Lathkill Dale. A narrow, wooded and rocky section, where some of the crags lining the narrow valley sides have crumbled to scree, opens out very suddenly into a lovely grassy limestone dale. Then a short but steep pull up Cales Dale with an exciting set of natural limestone steps leads back through a farm and country lanes to the café.

This former blacksmiths is full of character, with musical instruments on the walls and a log fire in the front room. On summer days its award-winning ice creams are a well-earned pleasure; on cold days their pints of tea/coffee and breakfasts go down a treat.

Friendly, efficient staff

▶ The Old Smithy at a glance

Open: Daily, 10.00-17.00 weekdays, 09.00-17.00 weekends (may be earlier to close in winter – varies with demand)

Food and specialities: Homemade cakes to full meals. Award winning ice-cream. All day breakfast (and breakfast baps)

Beverages: Freshly ground coffee/range of teas served by the cup, mug or even pint; apple and orange juice, cans of soft drinks, Real Ale (Peak Ales Brewery), premium lager and wine

Outside: Picnic tables (café food only, please) and grassy village green that can fill up on a busy day

The Walk

1. From the **car park** turn left and follow **Chapel Street** out of the village, dipping down to a side turn to 'Sheldon'. Take this; then turn right immediately after the house on the corner, through a squeeze stile, onto a footpath to 'Lathkill Dale'.

2. This leads into the top of **Bagshaw Dale**. The path follows the valley floor at the base of several small pasture fields then bends left after a stile to a country lane. Cross this, on a slight dog-leg left then right, to enter the top of **Lathkill Dale** on a continuing wide green path.

Enter the **National Nature Reserve** (NNR) proper, then access land at a couple of gates about 20 metres apart, staying in the bottom of the dale. A third gate marks a sudden change in character of the dale. **Limestone crags** now tower above the narrow sides, with occasional big blocky scree slopes at the side where some of the once-towering crags have crumbled and fallen (or been quarried) away. The path gets increasingly narrow and overshadowed by woodland.

The beautiful splashes of purple lining the grassy vale are Jacobs Ladder (Polemonium Caeruleum or Greek Valerian), the county flower of Derbyshire. Although rare nationally, it grows profusely

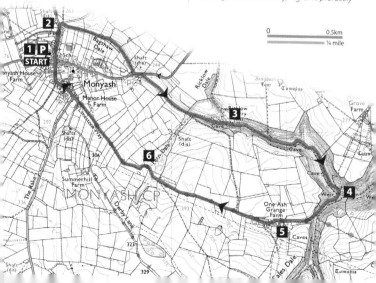

Jacob's Ladder flowers profusely in Lathkill Dale in early summer

in a few sheltered locations in the White Peak and Yorkshire Dales. Its Latin name indicates a possible connection with Polemon, a Graeco-Roman prince of Cappadocia in Roman times.

3. The sudden opening out of the view again into a **wider grassy dale** at a squeeze stile is something of a welcome surprise! As you descend to a rightwards bend in the dale, look out for a **large cave** on your right after which a side valley joins from the left and the valley sides grow taller and spread more widely from the valley floor.

In winter, a small torrent of water sometimes issues from this cave — it's the source of the River Lathkill. In summer the cave and its entrance are usually completely dry apart from a few damp bits of moss in the cave entrance. However the stream reappears above ground, usually producing a reasonable flow, by the time it reaches a footbridge lower down.

The clean gravel beds, soft silt at the riverbed edges and moderate flowing water form perfect conditions for brook lampreys, a rare eel-like fish. This primitive small

The path winds below lofty limestone crags in Lower Cales Dale

sucker-mouthed fish has no teeth and has been seen occasionally in the River Lathkill.

4. Soon after a gate, take a **bridge over the River Lathkill** to begin the ascent up the wooded **Lower Cales Dale**. After about 300 metres, fork rightwards (twice in close succession), go beneath an impressive **crag** then up a set of **natural limestone steps** to a **small cave**.

(Ignore the temptation of continuing up Cales Dale in access land — it can get impassably overgrown with nettles!)

A gate now leads into a grassy meadow flanked with **shallow limestone crags** and **farm buildings** ahead. Rise up steps

beside a **barn**, then along a farm track called the 'Limestone Way'. This merges with another track by an unexpected **grotto**, then bends left to a larger junction.

5. Follow signs to 'Monyash', turning right and right again to leave the farmyard. A **stony track** leads through a wide gate near a large tree stump. Follow the wall-line uphill through a long grassy field, crossing to the other side of this wall for the next couple of fields, bending right and uphill to a gate in the far corner.

6. Turn left through this into the shallow dry valley of **Fern Dale**, and follow the

drystone wall to a **walled lane**. Turn right at two junctions on bends and past the lovely **Fere Mere**. Go straight over a crossroads by the **village green** — the **café** is just ahead on the right.

Once refreshed, continue up **Chapel Street** to return to the **car park** to complete the walk. ♦

Unexpected Pond?

Monyash has a surface pond, which is very unusual for a limestone area — where water normally slowly percolates through the porous rock, creating caves and underground streams. But here, an overlying layer of clay allows the limestone bedrock to hold surface water. In fact, the village's listing in the Domesday Book was written as Maneis — meaning the 'village of many ponds' (there were five originally). Now only the pretty Fere Mere remains.

Mouth-watering vegetarian platters and superb salads at the Butterfly House

NEW MILLS

Butterfly House at the Torrs

Explore New Mills' hidden 'Park under the Town' with its amazing suspended walkway

What to expect:
Riverside paths, suspended walkway over a deep ravine, canalside, wetland and field paths

Distance/Time: 6.5 kilometres/4 miles. Allow 2½ hours

Start: Torr Top Street car park, New Mills (Pay and Display)

Grid ref: SK 000 854

Ordnance Survey Map: Explorer OL1 The Peak District: Dark Peak area, *Kinder Scout, Bleaklow, Black Hill and Ladybower Reservoir*

Café: The Butterfly House at The Torrs, 34 Market St, New Mills, SK22 4AE | 01663 741836 | www.facebook.com/TheTorrs

Walk outline: There's a watery theme to this walk as you descend into a narrow hidden ravine, then follow the Rivers Goyt and Sett to the Peak Forest Canal. A short walk on tracks and lanes leads to Hague Bridge, then some pleasant wetland paths. Finally, the walk takes you along the ingenious Millennium Walkway suspended on metal struts high above the valley below, before heading back up to that well-earned cake.

An artisan café with quirky architectural features and furnishings. Vegans, vegetarians and meat-eaters are all catered, and it's licenced for occasional music evenings. There's a great display of home-made cakes and some unusual Persian special dishes too.

Butterfly House sign

▶ Butterfly House at a glance

Open: 9am-4.30pm Thurs-Sat, 10am-5pm Sun, all year

Food and Specialities: All food is home made; fabulous choice of cakes. Their menu changes every week but always includes, pies, quiches, soup, tartins and oatcakes. Wheat-free cakes available; vegans and vegetarians well catered for. Eggs Benedict a speciality on Sundays

Beverages: Freshly ground coffee, range of speciality teas, hot chocolate; fizzy soft drinks (Fentimans and San Pellegrino, the elderflower is lovely on a hot day!). Locally brewed beer from Rock Mill, Torrside and Wincle breweries, wine and spirits

Outside: A couple of small tables at the front

White waterlilies and other water plants in the Hague Bar wildlife pond

The Walk

1. From the **Torr Top Street car park**, head towards the main street, following signs for the 'Heritage Centre'. Cross **Union Road** and take a **cobbled path** beside the **Heritage Centre**. This becomes concrete steps and descends towards the **River Goyt**. (Don't take the steps by the Torr Top car park — a rockfall has closed the path).

2. At the base of the steps, turn left towards **Torrs Hydro** and continue under the **Union Road bridge**. *The small bridge just before the former Torrs Mill, which was destroyed by fire in 1912, was once the main river crossing point; it was a long and steep route that went down and then up the valley sides.*

Pass **Torrs Mill**, cross the **River Sett**, then head below the scenic double-decker **Church Road bridge**. You're now following the **River Goyt** upstream on the **Goyt Valley Way**, passing former mill-workings on the way.

A modern building within the ruins of the Torrs Mill houses a modern day, local community owned, micro-hydro project. It is based on a simple but highly effective 'Archimedes Screw' (dubbed 'Archie' by local schoolchildren) and the clean renewable energy is sold to the local Co-op supermarket. The money funds a local community grants programme.

3. As the river valley bends right, join a wider **gravel track**, still heading upstream in the valley bottom. Just after **Goytside Farm,** turn right to stay on the **Goyt Valley Way**. This narrows after a farm entrance then bends sharply across the River Goyt on a **footbridge**.

At just 15 miles long, the Goyt Valley Way is too short to be a long-distance path —

but its connections to the Longdendale and TransPennine Trails offer onward long-distance routes across the Pennines. Goyt Valley Way runs from Vernon Park in Stockport to Longdendale.

4. Detour briefly into the **Goytside Meadows** then head uphill on the path and above the pastures. Rise up more gently beneath the **canal embankment** to the canal **towpath**. Walk ahead with the canal on your left.

5. At **Bridge 27** turn right onto stony **Lower Greenshall Lane** and descend steeply to a road junction on a hairpin bend. Head right, downhill, and cross the **Hague Bridge**.

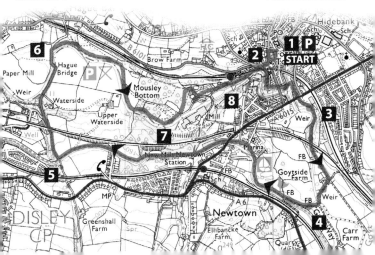

A walker admiring the view from the dramatic, elevated Millennium Way

6. Within 100 metres, turn right, towards the 'Torrs Millennium Walkway' and follow the river downstream, keeping it on your right. It's worth taking a brief detour left to see the lilies on **Hague Bar wildlife pond**. Continue, keeping close to the riverbank, to enter **Mossley Bottom Local Nature Reserve**.

7. Follow the **riverside path** past a **waterworks building**. Then veer left onto a path through woodland following 'Goyt Valley Way' signs; these take you right at a path junction, past a building and briefly onto a lane before bending left onto a shady footpath. Cross a road and continue in the same direction above the river. A wide path now leads down to the river valley towards the **Millenium Walkway**.

The Millenium Walkway is an elegant steel walkway clinging to the vertiginous sides of the sandstone gorge. Installed in 1999, it enables passage through the Torrs on foot and connects up a missing link on the Midshires Way (a 225-mile long distance path linking the Ridgeway to the TransPennine Trail).

8. Follow the riverside path, ignoring a turn right where the **Goyt Valley Way** leaves our path, and continue past **Torr Vale Mill** on the **Millennium Walkway**. Bend round beneath **Rock Mill**, then turn

sharp left back on yourself to rise steeply up a set of **concrete steps**. Pass the **New Mills Heritage Centre** and turn right on **Rock Mill Lane**. Cross **Union Road** and walk on past the **Pride of the Peaks pub**.

Continue past **Rock Street** (which leads to the car park) and head along **Market Street** to the **The Butterfly Cafe at The Torrs** on your left. Once refreshed, return to the car park to complete the walk. ♦

Industrial Heritage

New Mills began as a few workers' cottages built around a corn mill back in the 14th Century. It has since had a long industrial history, with coal mining, cotton milling, calico printing and bleaching industries all booming here in the 18th Century. The mills fell into decline in the 20th Century; and the Torrs lay derelict for over 50 years before being rejuvenated as 'The Park under the Town' in the 1970s.

Enjoy excellent coffee at the Edensor Tea Cottage

Edensor Tea Cottage

Explore the rolling hills and lesser-known parts of the Chatsworth Estate followed by a lovely riverside ramble

What to expect:
Estate tracks, rolling pasture, easy riverside paths beside the River Derwent

Distance/Time: 6.5 kilometres/ 4 miles. Allow 2½ hours

Start: Calton Lees Car Park (Pay and Display)

Grid ref: SK 258 685

Ordnance Survey Map: Explorer OL24 The Peak District, White Peak area, *Buxton, Bakewell, Matlock and Dovedale*

Café: Edensor Tea Cottage, Edensor, DE45 1PH | 01246 582315 | www.edensorteacottage.co.uk

Walk outline: The walk begins with a gentle ascent on estate tracks to Calton Houses and New Piece Wood. A short stand of woodland provides shade, then there's a lovely view followed by a descent through grassy meadowland to Edensor village. After the café, a gentle stroll leads across the road and alongside the River Derwent back to the start.

This former farmhouse is a bit like Dr Who's Tardis — seating more people than you would believe from the outside. They offer a very wide range of full meals but also good breakfast cobs, lovely home-made cakes, oatcakes and sandwiches for those wanting a smaller snack. A huge range of teas and coffees too.

Professional service

► Edensor Tea Cottage at a glance

Open: Daily; 09.00-17.00 weekends, 10.00-16.30 weekdays. Seasonal hours over Christmas; closed early January for annual holiday

Food and specialities: Full breakfasts and lunches, breakfast cobs, summer salads, great cakes, cream teas. Gluten free bread available, coeliac and vegan diets catered for

Beverages: Wide range of teas and coffees, luxury hot chocolate, wine, Peak Ales (Chatsworth's own brewery), cider, wide choice of cold drinks

Outside: Outside tables (café food only, please)

The Walk

1. From the **car park**, take the minor road past the **garden centre** to a junction on a hairpin bend. Fork right here (straight ahead), on a **bridleway** running along a gated track. Rise gently at first, then around a steep pair of hairpin bends to **Calton Houses**.

2. After the hamlet, the track becomes a lovely shady woodland **green lane**. Bend right then go through the righthand of a pair of gates. Fork rightwards on a good path beside a wall, go through a gate, then head diagonally across fields, aiming just left of a **hay barn** ahead. *Look to the right down the field for an unexpected Swiss cottage.*

3. Bend gently left through a gate onto a broad track through **woodland**. Cross over a **forestry track**, then down to a gate into **open parkland**.

4. Bend right then straight downhill towards a **waymarker**. The way meanders slightly around a group of widely spaced trees, but is always heading downhill. Follow a fenceline around the left side of a **conifer plantation**,

the church spire leading you down to the village, where the path is indistinct.

5. A waymarker shortly before **Edensor Church** guides you slightly left of the church to a gate. Descend steep **steps**, with a level link rightwards part way down, to gain the **village road**. Turn right along this, bending right around the church to the **Edensor Tea Cottage**.

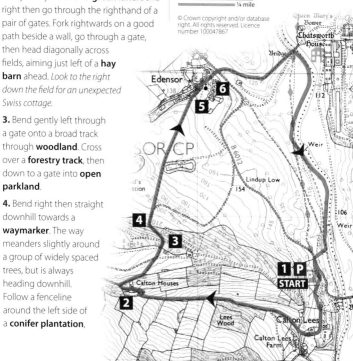

Chatsworth House sits in extensive, historic landscaped parkland

6. From the tearoom, turn right and walk down to the gate/cattle grid. Cross the main road through the estate; a path diagonally opposite leads down to a **bridge** across the **River Derwent**. Cross an estate car park road here, keeping to this side of the bridge.

7. Continue alongside the river through parkland, with great views of Chatsworth House across the water. Walk on past the **weir** to a **ruined mill**. Bend sharp right at the mill and head up to the road next to a cattle grid. Cross the road and turn left through a **blue gate** to return back to the **car park** at **Calton Lees** to complete the walk. ♦

Edensor village

The old estate village of Edensor originally stood beside the River Derwent. But after the 4th Duke demolished several buildings that were visible from Chatsworth House, the 6th Duke decided it would be better to remove the village in its entirety. It's said his indecision on what style to adopt for the new buildings lead to Edensor's oddly varied architecture. Apparently, the Duke simply commissioned a few of each building style offered by his architect.

Relaxing with tea and cakes in the homely Penny Pot Café

Penny Pot Café (National Trust)

A strenuous walk around the Edale edge of the Kinder plateau with an exciting high-level ford crossing

What to expect:
Rough hollow way, country lane, access tracks, open moorland, grassy descent.

Distance/Time: 9.5 kilometres/ 5½ miles. Allow 4½-5 hours

Start: Edale Main Car Park (Pay and Display)

Grid ref: SK 124 853

Ordnance Survey Map: Explorer OL1 The Peak District: Dark Peak area, *Kinder Scout, Bleaklow, Black Hill and Ladybower Reservoir*

Café: National Trust Penny Pot Café, Station Road, Edale S33 7ZA 01433 670293 | www.nationaltrust.org.uk/kinder-edale-and-the-dark-peak

Walk outline: A short stroll across fields leads to a steep climb up Ollerbrook Clough and The Nab onto the Kinder Plateau. There're great views from the edge over the Edale Valley with unusually shaped rock outcrops to add interest to the edge. An awkward ford at the main Grindsbrook headwater adds some challenge, then it's a final gentle ascent to Grindsbrook Knoll, and a quick escape down a track to the café.

When it's cold and wet outside, and their log burner is glowing brightly, the sofas in this homely café can be hard to escape from. There's a book exchange and home made cakes and snacks, too. The paninis are excellent, as are the cream scones and coffee.

A refreshing cup of tea

▶ Penny Pot Café at a glance

Open: Daily 10.00-16.30, plus early weekend opening from 08.30 May-Sep. Winter hours: (Nov-Feb) 10.00–16.00 Fri-Sun only
Food and specialities: Homemade and seasonal food. Hearty breakfasts, including breakfast baps, delicious lunches, locally made ice-cream and cakes. National Trust Farm specialities
Beverages: Freshly ground coffee, speciality teas, bottled soft drinks
Outside: Picnic tables outside, small garden area at the back

The Walk

1. From the **visitor centre car park**, head up the village road, beneath the **railway bridge**, past **The Rambler Inn** and on just past the **Moorland Discovery Centre**.

2. Take a footpath to the right, just opposite **Church Cottage**. Cross **Grinds Brook** and climb over an unusual **triple stile**. An intermittent stony track across two fields leads to a **farmyard**; keep a drystone wall on your right through the yard. Roughly 20 metres past **The Stables Bunkhouse**, take a

concessionary footpath on the left, by **Ollerbrook Barn B&B**.

3. This leads into cattle pasture; follow the field edge runnning parallel to **Oller Brook**.

Enter access land after three long fields, forking left to keep the uphill path just left of the brook. Roughly 200 metres on, the path veers away from the valley, rising diagonally across the hillside.

4. Bend around a good **viewpoint** on the nose of **The Nab**, then fork left and uphill on a **stone-pitched path**; avoid a descending path. Stay left at two forks

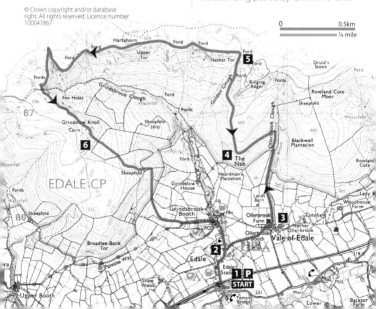

A walker carefully crossing Grindbrook's main headwaters

by cairns either side of a slight dip. Bend gently around the hillside, then rise on an increasing gradient across the hillside below **Ringing Roger**, the terrain gets rougher and steeper and heads towards a large **cairn**.

About 15 metres beyond the cairn, the path bends left to cross a usually dry headwater. **Stone flags and pitched steps** lead to a path junction. Turn left; the path becomes vague in peaty ground, as you rise diagonally up to the **moorland edge**.

5. It's roughly 2 kilometres to **Grindsbrook's main headwater**, a deeply incised inlet in the **plateau edge**. Keep the edge on your left all the way. There are intermittent sections of stone flagging, occasional detours across minor streams, and some vague paths through peat-hags and alongside rocky outcrops. Passing through a gate, the edge path continues past a couple more isolated rocky outcrops, then bends rightwards into a side-valley.

At the **main headwater**, there is a **ford** which can be awkward, but in summer usually provides only mild entertainment.

Looking out towards the Great Ridge from Ringing Roger

Alternatively an easier crossing takes a narrow path further up the side-stream. If fording, cross the stream-bed slabs, then inch left along a narrow ledge. A mildly eroding path then takes a **tall step up** to an **edge path**. Maintain your direction on this back out to the main valley, along to a second headwater (this one is easier to cross) then up a sandy rise by a large **cairn**.

6. Take care at this point to locate the correct onwards path: it's left of the more obvious stone-slabbed path cutting across moorland towards Kinder, but doesn't descend the Grindsbrook valley. Instead, the correct path continues along the edge above **Grindsbrook,** heading towards the **Knoll**. A strangely shaped **pinnacle rock,** about 50 metres in, helps confirm that you're on the right path. The path braids a bit just before the **grassy summit**; the leftmost path skirts around the top.

7. *At the summit there's a great view over Edale.* Roughly maintain your direction as you descend steeply down the far side. The **broad stony path** takes a line towards the left of a large grassy plateau, then steepens and bends into a slight hollow way. Leave access land by a wide gate and descend gently on a wide grassy line, bending left across fields.

Cross over an almost imperceptible stream at a junction with the **Pennine Way**, (it's more clearly channelled below), then through a gate which brings you down into the **village** opposite the **Nags Head pub**. Turn right and follow the village road downhill under the railway bridge. The **Penny Pot Café** is on the right towards the station; once refreshed, return to the car park on the left to complete the walk. ♦

Ringing Roger

Some great landscape names surround Edale, but what's the origin of Ringing Roger? One legend claims a packhorse trader found this spot a great viewpoint on the way to Edale. His name was Roger, but because he was bad at packing his ponies so their loads didn't jingle, he was nicknamed Ringing Roger. His favourite viewpoint was named after him. True? Probably not; the name's origins are lost in time, but it makes a good story.

Enjoy the lovely woodland setting at the National Trust's Longshaw Café

LONGSHAW LODGE

Longshaw Café (NationalTrust)

*Rolling moorland tracks make for a fairly gentle stroll
around historic lodges*

What to expect:
*Estate tracks and paths,
grassy moorland,
boggy in places, two
road crossings*

Distance/Time: 5.5 kilometres/ 3½ miles. Allow 2½ hours

Start: National Trust car park at Longshaw Lodge (main car park –
Woodcroft). Free for NT members. Otherwise Pay and Display

Grid ref: SK 266 800

Ordnance Survey Map: Explorer OL24 The Peak District, , White
Peak area, *Buxton, Bakewell, Matlock and Dovedale*

Café: National Trust Longshaw café, near Foxhouse, Grindleford
S11 7TZ | 01433 637904 | www.nationaltrust.org.uk/longshaw-
burbage-and-the-eastern-moors

Walk outline: Passing the historic lodge, the walk wanders
through a yew copse and rhododendron-lined paths down
to a lake. Head gently downhill across grazing land to a path
through the former Sheffield Plantation. This meets a footpath
rising up through open moorland to a track below the main
road. Continue across open moorland past White Edge Lodge,
then cross the road to an easy track back to the Lodge café.

*The Longshaw Café takes home-made to a new level with its own
kitchen garden providing ingredients such as herbs, rhubarb and
whitecurrants; other ingredients are also locally sourced. Large
communal seating area too.*

Fresh homemade scones

▶ Longshaw Café at a glance

Open: Daily, 10.30-17.00 in summer, closes at 16.00 in winter
Food and specialities: Homemade cakes to full meals. Home-made
scones and cakes a speciality. Staffordshire oatcakes, sausage and bacon
baps, specialities such as courgette and goat's cheese flan, home-grown
produce from the estate's kitchen garden
Beverages: Barista style and filter coffee, range of teas; soft drinks
Outside: Picnic tables (café food only). Views across Burbage Valley

The Walk

1. Head downhill from the **parking area** and go over a **bridge** into **woodland**. Cross an estate road towards the **visitor centre** and reach the **café** after just 50 metres. Turn right opposite this, taking a path signed 'Estate walks', that leads around **picnic tables** and then under a **ha-ha** below **Longshaw Lodge**.

Ha-has were a parkland feature that originated in France in the 17th Century, designed to stop wild animals from entering the estate house and gardens. They became popular in England in the 18th century as a way of excluding grazing sheep and cattle without spoiling the view.

Around the visitor centre look out for a seasonally-changing series of childrens trails such as the Boggart Trail. These add extra interest for younger visitors and aim to help more children enjoy free-roaming wild play in the outdoors. While they encourage plenty of jumping and running around, they also encourage learning respect for local wildlife habitats which may be sensitive to wilder play. This sensitivity is often seasonal, so look out for temporary signs, eg: when fungi is fruiting.

0	0.5km
	¼ mile

An easy, surfaced path skirts the lake near Longshaw Lodge

2. Go through a gate into a **stand of yews** and take a rhododendron-lined path to the right. Go through another gate and a grassy area with views over the **Lodge Lake** before bending down to the lake. At the lakeside, head left through a gate towards Yarncliffe; a grassy track leads gently downhill beside **Granby Wood** before merging left with an estate track. *The wood is named after the Duke of Rutland's son, the Marquis of Granby.*

3. Cross a stream **bridge** and head roughly straight ahead towards a grassy vehicle track. Almost immediately fork

right onto a fainter wide grassy path at the edge of bracken. Cross a couple of tiny streams; the path bends gradually rightwards and slightly downhill, but stays well above the sharp drop right to a **former quarry**.

As you cross this section of the Sheffield Plantation, you are crossing a Scheduled Ancient Monument containing evidence of a very early (medieval, or possible even pre-historic) enclosed field system, although the evidence is hard to spot to the non-trained eye. The Plantation itself came later (1823 to 1856); little now remains of this, and the National Trust is in the process of removing

Looking back towards Longshaw from near Wooden Pole

conifers and further restoring native trees to the landscape.

Pass through a gate; the path now roughly contours at the top of denser woodland. Shortly after a brief view of Grindleford station far below and just as the path begins to descend more steeply, fork left and through the wall to a fainter path. This roughly contours by the wall line, then leads across open bracken-covered moorland as the wall line veers left.

4. After roughly 200 metres, ignore a tempting looking fainter path left, cross a slightly awkward drain, then meet a wide grassy path. Take this uphill towards woodland, joining a line of **stone flags** shortly before the field top.

5. Take a stile over the wall then fork right twice to gain a gravel track, which leads to a busy road. Cross this and head slightly leftwards to gain a wide grassy track on the far side. This leads uphill with a pair of sweeping bends left then right to **White Edge Lodge**.

6. Pass right of the Lodge then follow the continuing gravel **estate track** back to the road just before a junction. Cross both forks of the road, taking a white-gated path shortly before a tall **wooden pole**. Fork left to traverse well below the pole on a grassy track, then merge with

a path from the left which becomes a gravel track.

7. Approaching walled woodland, the main path bends left and through a gate. Stay on this towards the **visitor centre**

— turning right to return to **Woodcroft car park** or left near the bottom to visit the **café** to complete the walk. ♦

Lodges and dodges?

This walk passes two historic lodges. Longshaw Lodge was a former hunting lodge built by the Duke of Rutland to entertain his grouse-shooting guests. White Edge Lodge was the former gamekeeper's cottage. The Dukes of Rutland had a history of refusing walkers right of access. But when death duties forced the sale of the estate, a group of walking activists purchased it and gifted it to the National Trust. Ironically, it is now one of the most popular walking areas in the Peak District.

Enjoy friendly service at the Roaches Tea Rooms

UPPER HULME

Roaches Tea Rooms

The Roaches boast stunning views over Staffordshire and the Churnet Valley

What to expect:
Steep slopes, rough pasture, and a steep country lane.

Distance/Time: 8 kilometres/ 5 miles. Allow 3-3½ hours

Start: Layby opposite The Roaches Tea Rooms (or other laybys further up the road)

Grid ref: SK 007 612

Ordnance Survey Map: Explorer OL24 The Peak District, White Peak area, *Buxton, Bakewell, Matlock and Dovedale*

Café: The Roaches Tea Rooms, Paddock Farm, Roach Road, Upper Hulme, Leek ST13 8TY | 01538 300345 | www.roachestearooms.co.uk

Walk outline: From the café layby, there's a short walk up a country lane to grassy meadowland. Rise up sharply between gritstone outcrops to a great view, then meander through dappled woodland. Another short rise leads to the undulating ridgetop path. Beyond a small pool on the ridge, the path rises gently to a trig point. A quick descent on a wide path and country lane, it's an easy descent back to the start.

The interior snug (with a welcoming log burner in winter) is perfectly complemented by an airy conservatory and patio with stunning views over the Tittesworth valley. The Staffordshire oakcakes are a particular speciality, as are the home-made scones.

Tea and cake

▶ Roaches Tea Rooms at a glance

Open: 09.00-17.00 every day (Mar-Oct), 09.00-16.00 (Nov-Feb)
Food and specialities: Homemade cakes to full meals. Home-made scones and cakes a speciality. Staffordshire Oatcakes, all-day breakfast. Gluten free menu available
Beverages: Wide range teas including green and herbal; freshly ground ethical coffee; soft drinks, wine, beer
Outside: Patio and conservatory with views over Upper Churnet Valley

The Walk

1. Start from the **layby** opposite the **Roaches Tea rooms**, with the café on your left, and head up the quiet country lane below the impressive crags of **Hen Cloud**, a smaller gritstone outcrop just south of The Roaches.

As you pass a driveway to Roaches Hall imagine the scene some 80-90 years ago. When the Brocklehurst family housed a thriving small private zoo in its ground. Its most well-known former inhabitants were the wild free-roaming wallabies which escaped during the Second World War, after Courtney Brocklehurst was killed fighting abroad. It was thought they had finally died out in the 1980s, but occasional sightings have occurred since — with 2015 the most recent.

2. Take a path leading up from the lane into the **valley between Hen Cloud and The Roaches**, following a drystone wall on your right. It's not access land just yet, so ignore more than one tempting green diagonal grassy path to the left. As you reach a gate in the dry-stone wall, turn left and head away from it to a corresponding gate in the far wall on your left where **access land** begins.

3. Rise up between the rocks on a **wide stony path** then through an **old gateway**. The path soon leads you under some crags and through lovely shady **woodland** to a path junction on the edge of woodland. Turn right and uphill, another well-made stony path leads to the **top of the outcrop**.

A carved stone plaque here celebrates the royal visit in 1872 of the Prince of Teck and his wife the Princess of Cambridge,

Hard gritstone helps shape the distinctive landscape of Hen Cloud

whose daughter Mary would eventually become Queen when she married Queen Victoria's son, George V. A rock chair was carved for the princess in one of the gritstone boulders and it was reported at the time that she displayed 'capital mountaineering powers' in the steep climb up a rocky staircase to reach the chair on the edge.

4. A well-maintained **edge path** now runs the length of the rising ridge to the white **Ordnance Survey Trig point**, some 1.2 kilometres distant, ignoring

any narrower side-tracking paths. At the start, it roughly follows a low drystone wall, although this fades away to peat in a few places and is soon left behind, near **Doxey Pool**.

In 2018 a large peat-fire swept across the moorland east of The Roaches causing widespread devastation. Staffordshire Wildlife Trust (who manage the Roaches Estate) have put significant effort into restoring the habitat, including artificially blocking some moorland drainage ditches over the 2018-19 winter period to help

Low evening light illuminates the dramatic gritstone scenery of the Roaches

moorland wetland plants recover more rapidly.

5. Towards the **trig point**, the path curves briefly away from the edge and rightwards between two clear bands of rocks. It now runs briefly below a layer of rocks and appears to fade, either follow a few metres of narrower path or trust the grip of the rocks and walk up the stone ramp to regain a wider path (still below a band of rocks first to the left, then the right as you cross a barely noticeable gap in the rock line).

On the summit ridge, the views are fabulous. On an exceptionally clear day it is said you can see as far as Snowdon in Wales, but great views over the Cheshire Plain and Tittesworth Reservoir are more usual. To the right are typical Staffordshire moorland plants such as cotton grass and bilberry, while in the sky above you, look out for peregrines. Between April and June they nest on the crags, and can dive at 120mph while stooping for prey.

6. From the trig point the ridge line opens out onto a **broader plateau** with more individual boulders than long vertiginous lines of crags, and begins to drop away down the now gentler left (west) edge. Below the main area of boulders the path becomes first pitched then stone-slabbed across heather.

Stone pitching returns once again as you descend to a country lane at **Roach End**.

7. Turn left onto this lane, cross a **cattle grid**, and stay on it all the way back to the **café**, some 3.5 kilometres distant. The lane enjoys great views back to the Roaches on your left and over the Meerbrook valley to your right. Continue through a gate, and keep straight ahead at a junction with a minor road. Return to the layby to complete the walk. ♦

Doxey Pool

Local legend claims this small pool high on the ridgeline is either bottomless or connected to nearby BlakeMere (on Morridge) via an underground passage that never dries out. A more sinister myth is that of Jenny Greenteeth, a malicious water sprite whose singing lures unsuspecting walkers to their death in either of the two pools. Or perhaps that's just a story to scare kids from playing in deep water, for the area can become disorientating when fog descends.

The Three Roofs Café is tucked below Peveril Castle at Castleton

CASTLETON

Three Roofs Café

A lovely limestone dale leads to undulating upland pasture and the 'broken road' under 'Shivering Mountain'

What to expect:
Varied limestone terrain, steep dale, upland pasture, collapsed hillside road, bouldery crags

Distance/Time: 9.5 kilometres/ 5½ miles. Allow 3½ - 4 hours

Start: Castleton Visitor Centre Car Park (Pay and Display)

Grid ref: SK 149 829

Ordnance Survey Map: Explorer OL1 The Peak District: Dark Peak area, Kinder Scout, Bleaklow, Black Hill and Ladybower Reservoir

Café: The Three Roofs Café, Castleton S33 8WN | 01433 620533 | www.threeroofscafé.com

Walk outline: Head out past Peveril Castle and up Caves Dale on the Limestone Way, then cross the plateau above the Hope Valley, past Rowter Farm. Then traverse Mam Tor's moorland flanks. There's a short detour to the Odin Mine and some boggier ground by the Odin drainage stream (Odin Sitch) on the way back to the café.

The pavement terrace is perfect for people-watching, with a cider in hand and a slice of freshly baked cake, a clotted cream scone or a vegan brownie on the table. There's plenty of space indoors, plus full meals, gluten-free ice cream, and a wide range of soft and hot drinks.

Tempting home-made cakes

▶ Three Roofs Café at a glance

Open: Daily 09.30 -16.30 Mon-Fri, 09.30-1700 Sat-Sun. Closed Christmas Day, New Year's Day

Food and specialities: Wide range from soups and sandwiches to full lunches. Locally made ice-cream, home-baked cakes and cream teas. Vegetarian and gluten free. Breakfast baps until 1pm — or later if quiet

Beverages: Wide range - freshly ground and barista-style coffee, range of speciality teas, hot chocolate, bottled soft drinks including J2O and Fentimans range, milkshakes, premium lager and cider

Outside: Several tables outside on Castleton's popular main street

The Walk

1. From the **visitor centre car park**, turn left onto the main road and down to the **Bulls Head pub**. Turn right onto **Castle Street**, then bend left and gently uphill past a small **triangular green**. As **Market Place** becomes **Pindale Road**, take a bridleway right towards 'Cave Dale'.

This leads almost immediately through a 'roofless cave', then up **Caves Dale** on the **Limestone Way** (here a stony limestone track). This is rough limestone at first as it

rises up through a narrow valley beneath **Peveril Castle**, later becoming grassy and easier going as the valley widens and levels out.

2. Bend right at the end of a short section of permissive **open access land**, and go through two gates some 200 metres apart. At the **second gate**, make sure you *remain on the bridleway*, which follows the continuing line of the incoming path (bending gently left and uphill), and *not* on the farmers path straight ahead. Roughly 500 metres later, bend left and head through a sheep pen leading to a junction with a **stony track**.

Walking up Cave Dale near Peveril Castle, Castleton

Turn right onto this track, now parting company with the Limestone Way. Go through a gate and stay on this track to the road end past **Rowter Farm**; it bends right at a junction with a bridleway early on.

3. Take a slight dog-leg right, then left, across the road and onto a track leading towards Mam Tor. This goes over a slight rise, then just before the gate back onto the road, turn right, almost back on yourself, on a **wide unwaymarked grassy path**. Cross the road, then take a line aiming just left of distant trees over an undulating field. Go through a gate by these trees and follow the wall line to a **farm**.

As you reach the **farmyard gateway**, turn sharp left over trackless ground. A vague track then forms just this side of a small valley, arcing gently right along the rim, then down the valley side, before bending right and through a gate to pass the **Blue John Cavern buildings**. Follow the tarmac access road across the shallow valley, rising steeply to the head of the **old Mam Tor road**.

Cave Dale and Peveril Castle above Castleton

Built as a turnpike in the 1820s, Mam Tor Old Road was the former main road between Sheffield and Manchester. But regular landslips meant is was in constant need of repair right up until the 1970s. But by 1977, one landslip too many meant the council gave up repairing it and it was closed permanently to traffic in 1979. Now it forms a wonderfully broken and misshapen tarmac path which mountain bikers and walkers alike love to use.

4. Turn right along the **Mam Tor Old Road**. Where the public road ends at a **turning circle**, continue through a gate into access land and down across a small boggy bit onto the remnants of the old road. Follow the eroded tarmac around a sharp, righthand, hairpin bend, then down to the lower public road access.

5. Detour to the right through a walkers gate to explore **Odin Mine** (watch out for the crags and boulders at the entrance to a side cave).

Then about 30 metres down the road, just beyond the bus stop, fork very sharp left and through a gate down to the 'Crushing Circle' This crosses a couple of shallow headwater valleys before bending right on a hawthorn lined path, aiming directly towards the Castleford cement works chimney.

6. Leave the open access land just before **Knowlegates Farm**, where the path detours down steps and through gates around the **farmhouse** before returning to its line through grassy fields. Cross the small **stream**, then roughly follow the stream edge. Cross a tarmac farm track then bend right on a wide grassy track to a **snicket gate** leading to the main road. Turn left and walk back to the **café** and **visitor centre** to complete the walk. ♦

Slip, sliding away ...

Mam Tor is popularly known as the 'Shivering Mountain' because of its curious underlying geology. Unlike most of the Peak District which is either dark, hard, impervious millstone grit or well-drained, porous, white limestone, Mam Tor is formed of shale. This fragile mudstone is unstable and prone to intermittent rotational landslips and regular debris flows. In fact, the mountain has been slipping and sliding for more than 4,000 years.

Useful Information

Visit Peak District & Derbyshire
The Peak's official tourism website covers everything from accommodation and special events to attractions and adventure. **www.visitpeakdistrict.com**

Peak District National Park
The Peak District National Park website also has information on things to see and do, plus a host of practical details to help you plan your visit. **www.peakdistrict.gov.uk**

Visitor Centres
The main Visitor Centres provide free information on everything from accommodation and transport to what's on and walking advice.

Bakewell	01629 816558	bakewell@peakdistrict.gov.uk
Castleton	01629 816572	castleton@peakdistrict.gov.uk
Moorland Centre, Edale	01433 670207	edale@peakdistrict.gov.uk
Upper Derwent	01433 650953	derwentinfo@peakdistrict.gov.uk

Rail Travel
Several railway services cross the National Park:

Hope Valley line

Derwent Valley line

Manchester to Buxton line

Manchester to Glossop line

Manchester to Huddersfield line (Transpennine express)

Information is available from National Rail Enquiries on 03457 484 950 or **www.nationalrail.co.uk**

Bus Travel
The Peak District's towns and many of the villages are served by bus. Information is available from Traveline on 0871 200 22 33 or **www.traveline.info**

Weather
Online weather forecasts for the Peak District are available from the Met Office at **www.metoffice.gov.uk/public/weather/mountain-forecasts/peak-district** or the MWIS can be more specific – **www.mwis.org.uk/english-welsh-forecast/PD**